Be H
Be Wh...
Be You!

Made
Whole

Made Whole

Whole

"A Woman's Journey from Painful to Purposeful"

YAHSHIKIAH "YAH" HUGHES

Praise for Made Whole

"'Lady Yah' gives heartfelt and real advice from her own personal trauma to help those who are struggling with living up to their full potential. Lady Yah wants you to break free from the emotional chains of the past and walk into the greatness that God has designed for you." -*Jackie Gardner, Author & Writing Coach*

"The author's ability to captivate the reader as well as walk the reader through a step by step process of healing and victory is profound" - *Tiffany T. Jones, Project Manager & Community Activist*

"The book is captivating, authentic and I was encouraged and inspired by the author as she demonstrated transparency in her effort to reach the masses. A must read" - *Ray Taylor, Pastor & Visionary*

"Educator, Mentor and Pastor Yahshikiah Hughes has hit a home run with "*Made Whole ~ a woman's journey from painful to powerful*." With a powerful mix of storytelling and inspiration, readers can feel the pain in her tribulations while learning from and rejoicing in her triumphs and lessons learned. A must read for anyone looking to learn how to break through and receive God's best" - **Rhett Burden, Author/Educator/Speaker**

"Every word stood out and showed the in-depth feelings of a woman who was vulnerable and weak. I like how after each story, nuggets of wisdom & valuable lessons are shared with the reader for reflection. I felt connected with the author and was able to share in her pain & victories. This is a must read if you want to be **Made Whole** through God and desire to be healed from your hurt and pain." - **Sorena Eaddy, Author/ Speaker and Minister**

Written by Yahshikiah Y. Hughes

Cover Design by Raheem Dade of RD Design Co.
Photo by Michael Nichols (Nichols Photography)

Edited by Celeste Blake

Unless otherwise indicated, Scripture quotations in this book
are taken from the HOLY BIBLE, NEW INTERNATIONAL
VERSION.

Dedication

To the young lady lost, confused and trying to find her way, this book is for you. To the woman who is paralyzed by the daunting events of her past, this book is for the young lady inside of you who needs to move on, push through and seek completeness. My prayer is that the contents of this book will ignite the fire inside of you to push through the pain, confront the past and begin walking onto the path of purpose that God has promised you.

First and foremost, I thank God for everything. Without You, I am nothing. Thank you for your healing, deliverance and for using my life to show your redeeming power. Your grace and mercy is why I am forever grateful.

Kevin Sr., this book would not be possible without you. Your love and support has challenged me to grow, to follow my heart and to step out on faith. I am beyond blessed to have such an amazing man of integrity, strength and greatness as my husband and friend. My prayer is that when my time here on earth is up, you will say that I WAS ENOUGH. I love you beyond my heart and into the depths of my soul.

To my KJ, being your mother has been the most rewarding and fulfilling job I have ever had. Because of you, I am a better woman, you taught me to love beyond myself and to give even when I did not know I had anything to give. I love you beyond words and I am proud to be your mother. YOU ARE THE BEST SON EVER.

To my princess Karsyn, I pray that you only have to read this book as a form of support for mommy and not because you EVER thought that you were not worthy. My life's journey as a woman and all that I endured made sense the moment you were born and I pray that everything that I went through was to make you the BEST WOMAN ever. I love you more than you will ever know and know that you will always be ENOUGH.

Dawn. Thank you for showing me what true friendship is. You were there when I did not think I was enough. Your continuous support of me no matter the venture, makes my heart smile. I am grateful that God saw fit to give me a "bestie" in you. You inspire me in more ways than you know.

Celeste. My friend, my "*chica*" and now my **Editor**. I knew the moment we met in Accounting class, that we'd be not only friends but we would do great things together. Well greatness is upon us. You are such an amazing wordsmith. Thank you for being you, for catching the vision and making this project life-changing. I love you and let's do this again real soon.

To every woman (far too many to name) that has helped to shape me, deposited into me, encouraged me, prayed for and with me, fed me, wiped my tears away, listened, corrected and loved me during every stage of my development - THANK YOU! I am the woman I am today because of you. Continue to inspire, encourage and help others reach their potential. "I am because You are". I vow to pay it forward.

And finally, to my family and friends, I love you and I thank you for always being there for me, for supporting me, for accepting me and allowing me to be *me*. On this journey to become *whole* some of you did not understand what was going on, but I thank you for respecting and loving me beyond what you saw or understood.

I love you and may God bless you always,

Yahshikiah

Content

Introduction

Never in a million years did I see this, writing a book, sharing my pain and being in a healthy enough place to even verbalize my journey. This book was birthed out of my experience of overcoming, out of my process and out of my pain. My desire is that you read these words with intent - intent to push through your pain, intent to give healing a try, with intent to come out of this journey in a new place – a place of love, adoration and acceptance of yourself. My story may be different from yours but I know that the HOPE, FAITH and OVERCOMING is the same.

By definition to be "**Made**" means to be *produced* **or** *manufactured* **by constructing, shaping, or forming.** "**Whole**" *is a thing that is complete in itself.* To arrive at a place of being MADE WHOLE is in fact a journey, one that comes with pain, tears, and a sincere ability to trust! Trust in God and in yourself to grow, heal and be set free.

There is a story in the bible (Mark 5:24-34) of a certain woman, who for twelve years suffered from a bleeding condition that no doctor could treat. She spent an enormous amount of money trying to find a cure. She tried everything: doctors, home remedies, to no avail. This unnamed woman was ostracized for her condition and during that time had been living in isolation. Her issues had become her identity. She lived for twelve years in emotional turmoil, then one day she hears of Jesus coming to town and decides to press her way through the crowd to get her healing. As soon as she touches Jesus' garment she was "**MADE WHOLE**". Instantly, she was healed of her pain both physically and emotionally. What astonished me with this story, was that she decided long before she pressed her way through the crowd that she would be well, that she was not going to stay in this condition. She made a DECISION even in her pain, that it was not her final destination.

Just as this woman had determination and faith to no longer live with her condition, I believe that every one of us with a little faith, determination and desperation, can get to a place of wholeness.

*"**Sometimes God redeems your story by surrounding you with people who need to hear your past, so it doesn't become their future**"*- Jon Acuff

Ever wonder what it means to be emotionally healthy? Like, really emotionally sound? I ask this question often because in my observations so many of us are not well emotionally. I started the quest for emotional wellness long before I knew what it was. I had a craving for something more internally. I couldn't quite explain it, but I knew it was missing.

We're often living life in an emotional fog, just going through the motions, not really in tune with our feelings. Emotional wellness involves the awareness, understanding, and acceptance of our feelings. Emotional wellness is a key element in maintaining a healthy balance in our lives and in our relationships. It is the ability to learn and grow from your experiences.

It is very important to become whole in your emotional life, as it allows you to accept how you are feeling. Once you accept your feelings, you begin to understand why it is you feel the way you do, and then you make a decision how you would like to act in response to those feelings.

Then, there's the notion that becoming or walking in wholeness is not available to all - that there are only a select few who are *whole*. We all desire to be whole, but so few of us are *truly* whole. Why? Because our issues, our pain and our past tells us that we are not deserving of being whole. We then settle for a life that is less than what God intended for us, less than who we are and what we are purposed to be.

The definition of WHOLENESS is to be restored, healed and recovered from a wound or injury. This last part is what I'd like to expound upon - the *aftermath* if you will. We've all suffered emotional wounds, wounds that we didn't treat properly, that we left open way too long and which may now be infected - infected with lies, doubt, fear and complacency.

The recovery process is critical whenever we sustain injuries or something traumatic occurs in our lives. When you are in an accident and your body is pained, there is a recovery process; the time in which you take to heal, replenish, receive treatment and recharge. We often miss the opportunity to walk in wholeness because we dismiss the recovery period. This book talks about the hurt, but also shares the journey to recovery, comfort, and the power of WHOLENESS.

This book is not a "tell-all" or an indictment on anyone, but it is *my story* of triumph and my journey of bravery, becoming whole and walking in purpose. It's my due diligence, if you will, that I inform you that this book is meant to ignite your fire to start, continue, or push through your process to become the best version of yourself that God has already promised you are meant to be.

Wholeness looks different of each of us, the journey will not be identical but the strength, resilience, reframing and courage is all the same.

Today I have to ask; how bad do you want it? Are you ready to risk it all to gain a new life? A life of purpose and power? Of Wellness and Wholeness?

My desire is that every word pierces through to the core of your heart and forever be etched in your spirit.

The Journey-

Being complete, content, and accepting of oneself is not anything that happens overnight. It is in fact a journey. A "Journey" is defined as the act of traveling from one place to another, a process or a course. To look at my life today, one might think that I always had a great life, and that my journey was one of greatness, but with any amount of greatness, come tests of faith and in my case, blood, sweat and tears. To arrive at greatness we must begin with a process. The woman you have come to know and see or have been acquainted with is not the woman and little girl I knew many years ago. For years I secretly wished someone would save me - save me from my "terrible life". Save me from the life I no longer wanted to live, the life I never asked for and the life that left me wounded. Some days I didn't wish for a saving grace but that God would just rid me of the pain, the anguish, and heartache. If that meant no longer living, then that is exactly what I wanted.

Between the ages of 13 and 25 I lived in complete turmoil, both internally and externally. I secretly battled with depression, low self-esteem and self-hatred. Unknowingly, just like the diseased woman from the bible story, I too suffered for twelve long years! Those twelve years were the most formative years of my life and all I can remember is constantly doodling on paper, "Why me Lord? Why don't the people who are 'supposed' to love me, NOT love me?" At that time, I didn't know that the pain, the issues, and the angst were all a part of my promise. I walked around identifying solely with my issues. I **became** my issues, because I only knew to believe what my situation dictated.

What is the purpose of this book?

"As soon as healing takes place- go out and heal someone else" - **Maya Angelou**

After spending many years feeling that I should be different from who I was, believing I should be smarter, happier, more confident, prettier and ultimately something and someone else, I came to realize that I was not alone on this quest to self-understanding. So many women struggle daily with acceptance, loving themselves and being able to walk in true healing and deliverance. After secretly living with my issues of low self-esteem and untapped potential for more than twelve years, I feel that I am finally FREE! With any form of liberation, freedom and newfound joy comes the desire to help others. I remember the first time I uttered the words "I am enough." It was at a tumultuous time in both my mental and spiritual life. I had just had my son and I struggled with who I was and what I could possibly offer him in such a state. How could I be the strong mommy that he needed, when I felt that even in his infancy he was potentially stronger that I was? I remember running into the bathroom every time I felt the urge to escape and the bathroom quickly became my "hiding place". What I thought was a place of refuge, was in fact a place where pain evolved, where damaging thoughts consumed me and the enemy had one on one conversations with me. On one day in particular, I escaped to my bathroom weeping and sobbing uncontrollably like a scene from a movie. The frustration and desperation I was feeling consumed my entire body. I was scared and angry but desperate to ease the pain. I cried out and pleaded with God to take the pain away, to help me get over myself and over the "this" I was going through. I was thinking, "I am a mother and I shouldn't be crying more than my five month old son, right?" In that very moment I felt a sudden sense of peace and reassurance. It was as if I had cried out all the pain and God came in and immediately replaced it with perfect peace. I stood up and looked in the mirror, surprised to see that the image staring back at me was the little girl I used to be. I said to her, "I am ENOUGH. I am not my past, I am not what happened to me, I am not what others say I am, I am strong, powerful, I am fearfully and wonderfully made, I am the apple of God's eye, I am victorious and I am ENOUGH!" From that moment on my strength was realized. Those words became a reminder for the dark days. And now they form the song of my heart, and I sing them out loud!

Now, fast-forward to a time when those words began to take on life within me. I began to walk bolder, my head held its own highness and I couldn't help but pour out confidence everywhere I went. I started to attract to me, those who wanted more but just didn't know how to get it for themselves. It started with a story, then a prayer and eventually I started to give out cards with sayings of inspiration on them. People loved the campaign, they declared it for themselves and began to walk in their own light...but still, I felt that something was missing. While I was inspiring others to walk in honesty and confidence, I wasn't being transparent. I only gave them the finished product but never the blueprint. They never got to see or even know about the dark moments of my life. They never received the tools to overcome what was missing in their lives. So after praying, fasting and a whole lot of pushing, I turned my pain, my problems and my heartache into purpose.

This very journey, is what needs to be shared. I'd like to share with you an array of tips, inspiration and meditation, scriptures and total transparency to help you start your journey of becoming a better you and ultimately being **Made Whole**.

The *Journey* Begins…

ONE

CRUMPLED

Most great things are discovered by accident. My love for writing came out of a dark place in my life. I started journaling to release my pain and put into words what my mouth could never say. I would sit every night and write questions on paper. Twenty years ago, I didn't know that those mountains of crumpled paper would be very symbolic to my life, my journey and who I am today.

1996 and 1997 were by far, the worst *years* of my life. I found myself pregnant, homeless, and abused. I hated everything about those 730 days, as they turned out to be the worst *days* of my life.

It was the beginning of my senior year of high school. It was to be the year of celebrations and endless possibilities, right? WRONG! For this very woman, it was any and *everything* but. The once deemed "life of the party" and high spirited young lady, found herself dark, depressed, and angry. No one could understand the shift and they couldn't pinpoint what occurred, but they knew I was *different*.

"Well of course I'm *different*," I thought. What I had just endured would make anyone act "*different*". If you'd been beaten daily for the past two weeks and had to cover up bruises so you and your siblings did not go into foster care, you'd be *different* too. If you found yourself raising your two brothers and working while your mother was in prison over your summer break, you'd be *different* too. If you were then thrown out of the house and literally became homeless, you too would be *different*.

You see, over the course of two entire months straight, this was my reality, my story and my life. When September came and school started back up, I suddenly found myself avoiding everyone because of a recent gift from my mother, a black and blood clotted eye. Quickly, sunglasses became my friend and I literally became "too cool for school".

My mother had just been released from prison in late August (this was possibly her third stint during my life), and was out all night doing drugs, getting high and needing more money – possibly the money I had tucked away in a tiny makeshift pocket of my underwear, but nonetheless, *my* money that I refused to give. I knew the drill, 'give her the money or get punched'. On this night, I chose to get punched. I chose to "stand up" for myself and give her a piece of my mind. Well, a piece of my mind landed me on the floor, eyes swollen shut, braids ripped out of my head and ultimately defeated. I was so immune to occurrences like this one after all, this was my reality. And so without a second thought, I got up, got dressed and proceeded to school that morning like any other day...or so I thought. As I made my way downstairs to leave, I was greeted once again by obscenities and the fist. This time, I had taken all I could take. I came up with a plan (in my head) that after school I'd pack up all of my things and leave. Well, I was too late. I was thrown out that very moment, but without any clothes, shoes or any of "my things" - only what I had on my back. Thursday, September 12, 1996 was the day, by definition, I became homeless, never to return to my mother's house again.

The next few months, I stayed between the homes of some cousin's, my sister and even a childhood friend. Though I had no permanent place to call my own, I was grateful for an occasional bed, couch, and or even floor to sleep on. This started a series of life altering events: some good, but majority of them bad – heartbreaking even, conceived from hurt, immaturity and the need to survive. Because I saw **no way out**, I began to simply adapt - adapt to a big world that little ol' me knew nothing of. What I did know was that this big world cared nothing about me, I had no place or business in it and so I became...a part of this world. Living, breathing and embracing worldly ways, I found myself in way too many situations that I was way too young (in both age and mentality) to have been partaking in. While all around I was quite immature, my body was not. I began attracting the wrong attention from people and ended up dating a man a little too wise, too old and too advanced for me. Suddenly, at the age of 17, I found myself pregnant.

Sometimes when we do not understand things beyond our maturity level and aren't equipped to handle what comes along with it, we find ourselves in dangerous, life-changing (and life threatening) situations. This was my very harsh reality...What could I offer a baby? I'd just finished high school three months prior, I had no job, no place to live, no true support system and the father of the child *loved* the idea of *me* but not enough to create a *family*. I knew it would just be me and this baby, but the crazy thing was, it was already "just me". Reality set in further. I couldn't feed myself, I was sleeping on someone's floor, and I didn't have money for a pack of gum! I knew I wouldn't be able to buy diapers, let alone all the other necessities it takes to care for and nurture a baby's life...At least that is what my mind and circumstances forced me to believe.

"Yes ma'am, I'm sure" was how I responded to the counselor at the clinic with tears in my eyes...But was I really sure? How could I be in a situation like this? I'm not sure if I was more hurt that I let myself down or that I sat there face-to-face with my reality. It was just me sitting there. No one was at the clinic but me. It was Labor Day weekend in 1997 and while I should have been in Miami "living it up" with my friends for our graduation trip, I sat there sobbing, making the hardest decision of my life. There was no one to console me, no one to help me through it, not even a ride home after such a procedure. Once again, it was just *me*.

So I pulled my "big girl" panties off and agreed to have the **life** sucked out of me. I heard the suction, I felt the pulling, I saw the jar with my *"life"* inside, still moving, still holding on! "Oh Lord! Can't I put it back? I think I made a mistake! Can't I just fight through this?" No. It was too late.

As I tried to pull myself up and off of the cold, hard table, I fell face first onto the floor. I laid there sad and helpless, with not so much as a Nurse around to assist me. Was this symbolic of what my life had become? Had I hit rock bottom? I had literally fallen and no one was there to *help me* up. Could I get back *up* from this? I laid there frantically, praying that God would step in and help me up. Through the tears I mustered up the strength to get

34

up- up from the floor yes. But was I strong enough to *get up* in life or would I just *give up*?

Something inside of me died that day. I lost a piece of my soul. I resented myself for not being strong enough, for not being smart enough and for succumbing to the world I so desperately tried to escape. Nightmares consumed me for the next few years. I had panic attacks often but I kept a smile on my face. I was still doodling on paper every day, "Why don't they love me? Why don't I love myself?" But then I'd crumple the paper. I'd hurry up and place it in my pockets whenever I'd hear people coming around. Those balls of paper had become my life, my release – they were *me*. Everything that was left inside of me was reduced to a crumpled up piece of paper. I'd check back often to see if the answers to my daunting questions would mysteriously appear on the paper. "No answer today… I'll try again tomorrow," I'd say. And so I did, but still, no answer. I asked, "Lord why aren't you answering me? Why would you give me this life? I'm wounded and crumpled just like this paper."

Then one day I looked down on the piece of paper I was doodling on and I wrote, "Why don't the people who are "supposed" to love me, *not* love me? Why God, would you put me in this?" And in a clear audible voice I heard, "CRUMPLED BUT NOT TORN"...*Uh, excuse me where did that come from?* I sat there nervous and anxious, desperately waiting for the voice to come again - for someone to jump out of the closet or something, anything! But nothing and no one appeared. And so I sat crying uncontrollably. I was crying from anger at my life, my reality and my situation...and on top of that I figured I had gone crazy too!

What I didn't know then, was that those four words were the words I would hang onto and would later use to save my life. Like my balled up and hidden pieces of paper, all I could feel was the pressure and the crushing of life...all I could see were the *wrinkles*. It was all too much for me. But God was telling me that even though I was feeling worthless, crumpled and *useless*, I could still be used in the spirit of *goodness*. Just as a crumpled piece of paper can be taken out of the garbage and be used for something more, so could I.

Although it may not be pleasing to the natural eye to read, the content is still clear and is just as powerful.

Today, as you read through my journey and all that has led up to these very moments in my life, know that it was for *my* good. Everything that crumpled me and broke me down, was so that I could share it with you and to show you the power of God. He is the only reason I didn't tear apart, that I am still intact, and that I am ENOUGH.

MADE MOMENT

Today, I can embrace the beauty in the *bending*, I am okay with being "*different*" and I am finally at a place of clarity and honesty. I can be totally transparent with myself and those who need a similar healing. Because my misery has become my ministry, my wounds have helped me to be a healer. I am a wounded healer, who has had many bumps, bruises and battles along the way, but it has all made me BOLD, BRAVE and BEAUTIFULLY BALANCED.

"…….But God was telling me that even though I was feeling worthless, crumpled and *useless*, I could still be used in the spirit of *goodness*"

God can use YOUR PAIN!

TWO

LIFE AFTER DEATH

I knew all about life in death from a biblical standpoint - allowing God to give you life in death, after all, Jesus died for us and we now have eternal life. But what I didn't know was that my life would benefit from the deaths I experienced. How could I find meaning in such a painful place? Most people never recover from the physical deaths in their lives and here I am using them to catapult me to my purpose. How, you ask? Let me explain.

It was December 16, 2001, and the day started like every other, with me spending the day with my brother and then going to work. I worked the second shift at a bank, while taking care of my younger brothers who lived with me. At the time, my oldest little brother was 17, the youngest was 7 and I was 21. We were doing okay for ourselves, considering that fact that I became the "parent" at such a young age. So my routine was to come home at midnight, get my youngest brother from the babysitter, check on my 17 year old and go to bed. Well, this night did not quite go as planned. My youngest brother was with my mother for the weekend so, I decided to hang-out with a friend. He was teaching me how to parallel park for my upcoming driver's exam. Because I worked the second shift, we couldn't do this until just around 12:30am. Practice was going really well, but my mind kept putting me somewhere else. Around 1:45am I felt an uneasy feeling in my spirit, an sudden nausea had overcome my body I couldn't explain it, but I told my friend to take me home, I needed to check on my brother. He persuaded me to call him instead. So I called - no answer. I kept calling and calling and around 3am I decided to leave because something wasn't right. Well, I was right. My brother had been killed at 1:48am. He was just 17! My entire life was wrecked. How could this happen? Lord, why? Why would you take the only constant thing from me? We were making it, it was hard, but I did my best! Lord, why? The days after that were a blur. I don't remember making the funeral arrangements. I don't remember the days before the funeral. The only two memories I have were:

41

walking into my cousin's home for an emergency family meeting, scanning the room and not seeing my brother...I remember asking where he was and the silence in the room told it all; The other memory was me at the funeral home, braiding his hair when he suddenly let out that "final breath" that everyone talks about. My life was numb, it was over, I could not focus, I could not think, I wanted out!! I was angry with God. After all the things we've been through, everything we survived, how could he take the only person who understood me, understood the pain, and understood the struggle? He was my life! How could I go on? What did I have to live for now? My goal was to get him out, to make him proud, to give him and our younger brother a better life. How now, when one-third of the equation was gone?

Life was hard - really hard - after this. As I tried to regain a sense of normalcy, I returned to work. One night on the job, one of my co-workers pulled me to the side. He said, "You may not want to hear this but, I think God removed everything from you so that you can focus on you, becoming a better you." EXCUSE ME?!?! I looked at him as if he had two heads and wanted to call him everything but a child of God!

But those words haunted me. What did he mean? How could God use *this* to help me become better? How could death push me to having a better life? I later realized that God used my co-worker to plant the seed and give me direction in my life. I didn't fully understand, as my pain had paralyzed me, so I wasn't operating in faith. I was numb but I decided that if I wanted to be any good to my youngest brother and family I had to go! I decided to apply to college and get away.

I stepped foot on the campus of UMES (University of Maryland Eastern Shore) at the age of 21, wounded, depressed and very guarded. Not knowing a single person, it was there that GOD began to transform me, to cleanse me and to rid my heart of all the pain. I was removed from all things familiar. There, I had no family, no friends, just me and my blind faith (what little I had). It was there that I dealt with the deaths of both my children, the one I aborted and the one that I was purposed to care for - my brother. It was there that I learned that sometimes God has to take things from you (death) to allow you to trust Him and give you a new direction (life). It was there that I learned how to be brave, and not to be afraid of the dark places in my life.

"It's only when we're brave enough to explore the darkness will we discover the infinite power of our light"- Brene Brown

This is a very vulnerable area for me, it's a place that I don't let many people see, and not because I am ashamed but because it's so personal and at the core of my healing. Being vulnerable is scary, almost as scary as being faced with death because you're naked – emotionally, that is. In order for you to truly walk in wholeness there has to be a period of death. For you, it may not be a physical death that God uses to bring life, instead

44

it may be time for you to "dead" a situation you might already be thinking about. Wherever and whatever that "dark place" may be for you, it's time to stop allowing it to become the definitive answer for what life is all about. You carry the light, so you must be willing to LIVE, radiate from it and keep it illuminated.

MADE MOMENT

Growing up, I was terrified of the dark. I'd imagine all types of scenarios around the dark. I'd see Freddie Kruger appearing from my closet. I'd suddenly feel something grabbing me from underneath the bed. I despised the dark. Then, one night I had no choice but to conquer my fear. As I laid trembling and my eyes wide open, I realized that I could see in the dark with no light. If I stood long enough to calm my emotions, I could focus and remember what it all looked like in the LIGHT!

While I miss my brother terribly, I know that it was in his death that God allowed me to live - live a new life full of purpose and power. I went from thinking I had nothing to live for, to wanting to leave a living legacy of hope, inspiration and resilience. The two most significant deaths in my life have catapulted me into my purpose. All because I decided to show up in the dark places in my life. Will you use your dark places to push you to LIFE?

"In order for you to truly walk in wholeness there has to be a period of death."

THREE

MIRROR IMAGE

Our reflection can sometimes be hard to look at in the mirror. When we stand and face who we really are - after extinguishing the facades and illusions of the day, and when we take off our masks and remove the pretenses – oftentimes it is just too hard to deal with. It's so much easier to *act* like we recognize the person staring back at us, because it's quite convenient to *be* the person we want people to see. But the mirror doesn't lie. It shows every ounce of who we are, even when it's foggy in our minds, the image is always very accurate. Embracing the mirror image is our "stand in your truth" moment - a moment of recognition that each of us should have in order to live a life of peace, truth and healthiness.

Subliminally, I was taught to embrace the mirror but only when I "looked and felt good" and to otherwise avoid the mirror at all costs when I wasn't at my best. This became my practice in both the physical and spiritual aspects of my life. The mirror had become my barometer of life. I literally used it to gauge who I was. Standing there, staring at my reflection caused me to be explicitly *real* and deal with the current pain, past hurts, life situations and whatever else God needed me to see to begin a change in me...I believed that I was damaged goods. The closer I looked, the more I saw the flaws, the damage, the residue. There were no masks, no illusions, just me and I did not like who I saw. The image that stared back at me *resembled* me, but I didn't know her.

For so long, I avoided my "moment". The moment when I could no longer use the mask or show my poker face or fake my way through...was my moment of truth. I had to stand there and take it. I had to be honest with who I was, not with what "they" did to me or what I did to myself, but what I was going to do from here on out! *I* had to have that tough conversation with *me*. With a long and loud sigh, I gave myself permission to 'not be okay' and to 'take my time healing, growing and changing'. I didn't beat myself up for walking past the mirror for so long and I didn't talk down to myself anymore. In fact, I completely turned that all around! I congratulated myself for no longer avoiding my image and for having the courage to finally look at myself in the mirror.

Although, the reflection in the mirror may be one you'd prefer to walk past, you must stop and really stare at yourself. Take an honest inventory of who you truly are. Yes, you're broken, bruised and may even still be wearing the scars of yesterday, but you are still standing! You are standing because of God, not in spite of Him. Even though you may be unrecognizable right now and you don't know when things will change, you must face you - the real you - the wounded and broken you that only you and God know best.

So stand in your truth, look yourself dead in the eye and say, "By his stripes I am HEALED! He has carried me through the darkest times and places. He was with me when I was too embarrassed before Him and ashamed. He loves me, accepts me, and knows me, so I need to learn love and accept myself."

Nothing you've done up until this very moment can change the love GOD has for you. He has seen you through it all. He knows every detail of your life because He created it. So take your stand in front of that mirror, stand in your truth, ask GOD to help you accept yourself. Stand in your truth today. Accepting your reflection will cause you to have a deeper connection with yourself and with God. There is real peace and serenity that comes with being open, honest and raw with ourselves. It takes strength to look at the image and say, "I want to change, I do not like what I see, I am better than what I have become." Grab your mirror and speak to the image you want to see, not the image you think you see before you now.

MADE MOMENT

It was totally necessary for me to stand and face the mirror while my truth was the image staring back at me. It was imperative that I stood there accepting where I was and who I was at that very moment. My truth ran deeper than what I was

51

seeing. It was about what I couldn't see, how I was feeling about me and how I allowed that negative voice inside of me to keep me enslaved for so long. My truth helped me to be authentic, transparent and powerful. I no longer have to hide or pretend and I give myself permission to be flawed. In that moment, I allowed God to step in and take over the healing process, because for so long I avoided it. I tried to hide instead of being healed.

FOUR

REJECTION MADE ME DO IT

"**W**hat did you just say?", I asked. He tried to cover it up with a cough, maybe to buy himself a few minutes to conjure up a lie or to somehow take it back. Did he just call me someone else's name? Did I hear what I think I just heard? Should I make him stop?

"Get up", I yelled. "GET UP!"

The crazy thing is, I'm not sure whether I was talking to him or to myself.

I can't really see much, darkness is surrounding me, I'm in his basement. How symbolic of my life this all is turning out to be. But I'm literally in this low, damp, dark, cold place. The place where numbness plagued me and emptiness pierced my soul. There I was giving the most precious part of me to someone who couldn't remember my name. Of all the times to forget...this is the time you chose. He was the same one who pursued me for months, walked me home, bought me gifts, spent countless hours on the phone whispering sweet everything's...and the moment I give myself to you, YOU FORGET MY NAME? Isn't this the part where you say my name? Or, you whisper in my ear and tell me how much you love me? At least, that is how I envisioned it playing out anyway. But there I was, feeling worthless, sad and disgusted, debating whether or not I should just "get up". My reality was that I was fighting for my life. But why? Why am I still fighting with "her" and her friends ("her" being Rejection, or "Re-Re" as I've come to refer to her as)? Of all the times for her to show up, of all the ways to manifest herself, *this* is how she hits me.

Rejection knows no bounds; it shows up at the most inopportune time and it feels terrible. Rejection communicates to us that we're not loved, wanted, worthy or valued. And guess what? We believe it. Rejection is the voice of our pain, and she speaks for all the wounded areas of our soul.

"The greatest damage rejection causes is usually self-inflected, just when our self-esteem is hurting the most, we go and damage it even further" - Guy Winch

So, how is it that I'd end up lying in bed, once AGAIN, with the man who called me another woman's name the first time we were intimate? How did we end up in a "situationship" for more than five years? *Dumb* you say? Nah, Rejection made me do it. Rejection made me believe that this was as good as it would get, that no one would ever want me and if they did, the same thing would occur. Re-Re told me this is what love looked and felt like, so I believed her (after all, we were friends for a very long time). But even in believing what was right in front of me, I battled with it internally. Deep down something was missing. I couldn't quite figure it out but the internal struggle was real. You see, some girls worry about the walk of shame or "the homies" finding out

55

what happened, but me, I worried about the condition of my soul. How was I "okay" after all of this? How did I just go back? Because I absolutely heard him loud and clear, but I didn't want to. I didn't want to deal with what it all meant. It meant she won again. Rejection had taken over and reared her ugly head once again.

She told me that love was beyond my reach, that I should keep my head down, that my past and my pain was all I would ever be and that this was as good as it would get. I knew Re-Re all too well, as we've had this feud for as long as I could remember and every time I thought I'd won, she'd hit me with another blow. The worst part was that I knew what she was capable of doing. We had been in this relationship since I was about eight years old. I didn't like her but I was used to being around her. You know that person you tolerate because you know what they're about? You see them for who they are and you just deal with them? It's such a sad truth.

Rejection told me that she and I would be best friends forever and again, I believed her.

The next time she showed up, I ended up in a holding cell, terrified that I would be incarcerated for "falling too hard for someone". Now, before your mind goes too far into the world of "I wonder was it...," let me just tell you, I fell for someone who loved me but loved another girl too. His "girl" got wind of our love and decided that one of us had to go...and of course, I had to go. "Go" as in, report his car, that's in her name, stolen and guess who just happened to be driving around in it that day? Ding! Ding! Ding! You are correct! "Miss Williams!" (my maiden name) the officer yelled, breaking my trance. "I need you to get up and come place all of your belongings in this bag." I hear him but I can't move. I am paralyzed with fear, shame, confusion and anger. Am I really being taken to central booking for a crime of passion? Did I really just get locked up for driving my "boyfriend's" car, that his "baby momma" had reported stolen? How can this be my life?

Why am I still battling this? I've been fighting this rejection spirit for a long time.

*"**Rejection sends us on a mission to seek and destroy our self-esteem**"- Guy Winch, Ph.D*

What a mission I was on. Rejection told me that in order to be loved I had to give something; and that "something" was my soul and my self-worth. I stayed in a spirit of rejection because I was committed to it emotionally and mentally. I had just as much invested in Re-Re as she had in me. For years I wanted different but I was not doing anything mentally, emotionally or physically to *be* different.

We stay far too long in our dark places because we're committed to those dark places. We believe the lies, we become numb and comfortable in that place and look up years later, lost and confused. Rejection is a wound that we continue to pour salt on, not allowing the doctor to treat it. We allow it to continue to burn and infect other areas of our body. When will you get up and get treated? When will you fight back? When will you fight for your sanity, dignity, wholeness, purpose?

I asked myself these same questions and then one day I mustered up the strength to finally "GET UP" and fight back. Getting up out of my pit was hard, and it took a lot of strength, both mentally and emotionally. Imagine climbing out of dark hole, underground, where no one can hear you, let alone lend you a hand. That's what exactly what I did. I climbed out, one rock at a time, one foot on top of the other.

Why? Why did I finally get up? Because I was scared - scared of how "okay" I was with all of this. I knew it was all wrong, and that it hurt, but my actions co-signed everything that rejection told me. I willingly indulged her. Rejection had a voice and I listened to her over and over again. I sat in that dark place scared and listened to all the voices of rejection, doubt, fear, and depression. I thought no one would "find" me. Who was supposed to find me anyway? And if they did, could they really help me? Rejection not only whispered to my soul, she screamed so loud and so much that I couldn't hear my own voice nor could I hear the voice of the Lord.

What has rejection made you do? How has it shown up in your life? You see, the crazy thing is that rejection makes us all do something that we're not too fond of, something that makes us question ourselves, our worth and our existence. Rejection manifests differently in each of us. She may have made her cameo appearance through designer bags, expensive shoes, friends and/or family, but she feeds us all the same lies - and they are all lies. Rejection works subtly to destroy your self-image and self-esteem. But she can be defeated.

A rejected person learns to use defense mechanisms to cope and to protect themselves. Oftentimes the rejected will conceal the fact that they have been rejected.

The three ways in which we handle rejection is:

    1. **Repression**- This form is when we bury the feelings alive, forcing the truth of rejection below the levels of awareness. We use this as a

subtle form of denial to protect us (at least we think we are protecting us).

2. **Rationalization**- We try to explain "why" or "explain away" the rejection. We make excuses for *what* has happened and *why* we are in this place. We try profusely to make sense of what occurred.

3. **Regression**- This is where we basically act like an "adult child" reverting back to child-like behaviors when dealing with our emotions. The rejection makes us literally act like we did the very first time it transpired in our lives. We can't move on from this part of our lives.

We've all managed our rejection in one, if not all, of these ways.

In order to conquer rejection, you must stand up to it. You cannot conquer what you do not confront. The reason you keep fighting it is because you haven't confronted it head on. You must silence rejection because it tries to separate you from God, yourself and others. Rejection isolates you and makes you believe that one mistake, or one painful moment or situation, is all that you are. Every lie, every bit of doubt, everything that she says to your soul, you must combat it with the truth. Redefine your relationship with rejection but most importantly you must redefine your relationship with you.

MADE MOMENT

The moment I realized that I had moments of rejection in my life but that I was not REJECTED, was the moment that I began to unlock my freedom. I spent so much time living in that dark place because I didn't know I could come out. I was in the prison cell of my pain. The bailiff had unlocked the door, opened it and sat the release papers on my bed. But I didn't move. Why not? Because, I was comfortable. I anticipated being free for a long time and finally I made a decision to not be afraid. It was the most liberating thing I have ever done. The confidence and acceptance is a result of listening to God and not my rejection. How much greater would your life be if you decided to believe what God says about you and not your rejected place?

"You cannot conquer what you do not confront"

FIVE

DRESS REHEARSAL

As little girls we were taught to "dress up". We actually played dress up with our mommy's, grandma's, sisters, aunts, cousins and friends. We dressed up our dolls, held tea parties and pretended to be princesses, doctors, lawyers, nurses, superstars, and mothers. While "playing pretend" was a normal childhood game, and casual pastime for most women, it created confusion- giving us a false sense of appearances. We were essentially taught that in order to escape reality, or to become someone else or to be someplace else, all we had to do was *pretend*. All we had to do was put on some fancy clothes and costume jewelry and we could be whoever we wanted to be.

Somewhere along the way (especially as adults), we've stopped pretending and have allowed our false appearance to become our *reality* and our *truth*! We've impersonated this fictitious character for so long that we too are now convinced.

As women, we have been doing a great job of *pretending*! Pretending has become our normal practice. We've been walking around lying to others and to ourselves, claiming that we are "perfectly fine" and that we are "blessed and highly favored". In truth, we have allowed our pain, hurt, and past experiences to overshadow who we are, steal our peace, and steal our joy and hope, so much so that we have gotten to the point where we are too afraid to look ourselves in the face! Instead we simply dress ourselves up! We disguise our wounds in expensive labels. We hold make-up plastered smiles on our faces to conceal the hurt. We even painfully strut around in high heels, hoping that our self-esteem might reach the same heights! We are so comfortable pretending, that we don't know who we are or what the truth is. We are living within the blurred lines.

Because the hurt and pain of facing who I really was and what had really occurred in my life was far too much to bear, pretending came very easy to me. I decided to audition for the leading role in my own mellow drama, **"It's Better to Believe the Lies You Tell, Than Face the Truth**". And guess what? I got the part. I was starring in a one woman show, chock full of *pretending*!

I can remember the day I stepped foot on my college campus. I vowed that I would be who I wanted to be. No one knew me there. They didn't know my name or my story. Why not create the life I always wanted and wanted everyone to know? So it began. My brother's mother who served as my mother figure was now my "Mother" and her husband, my "Father". And while they both graciously and lovingly took on these roles, I neglected to tell any of my college friends that they didn't actually birth me. When asked, I merely gave a glimpse of my life in Philly, and I never spoke of the things I had gone through growing up, after all, I was all dressed up for the part I was playing...Why not play it out completely?

You see, if I could be real with you, I was literally walking around *broken*. I learned to dress it all up, and very well might I add, but I was in pieces. Pieces of my torment were constantly surrounding me and I was reminded of those bits and pieces every time I looked in the mirror.

Who I saw staring back at me was always a "little female dog". My birth mother called me the meaner version of the term so much that I thought it was my nickname. I also saw the rejected girl whom everyone thought was "fast", and didn't want to be bothered with. My father planted those thoughts in my mind. He further planted a seed that said I would never be good enough for any man to stick around and love me. These things broke me down so much that I felt I had no choice but to dress up, play the part and pretend it never happened.

It was in college that I had to really learn who I was, and the more I tried to play the part, the more intense my pain grew to be. I eventually had to "stand in my truth" and began stripping the layers off, erasing all the lies I told myself and others. I learned to be okay with who I was, because after all, God created me this way and hiding who I really was did not honor God nor did it make the pain go away. As I began to strip down to my real and true self, I began to see me the way God saw me and the way he made me: beautiful, strong, loving, and *enough*. I was good enough not just for my college friends, but for myself. No longer did I pretend, rehearse or try to avoid me (and the mirror). I was no longer ashamed of my past or my parents. I began to allow God to help and heal me.

MADE MOMENT

When I got to my lowest point, which was when I couldn't look at myself in the mirror because of all the broken pieces, and the lies my past dictated, God stepped in. He showed me that it was all a process. A process that was intended to propel me to my purpose. He said to me, "*Daughter, where you are going in this life, I needed to purge you, I needed to test you and I needed to get you to a place in me that proved you did not need to count on others, but I cannot use you if you keep pretending and if you keep hiding who you are. I am waiting on you. Polish yourself up and show the world what I can do! I LOVED YOU in your broken state, I STILL LOVE YOU and I never took my hand from upon you."*

Those words resonated with me and I finally took the "dress clothes" off, stepped off the stage and began the healing process.

"......I eventually had to "stand in my truth" and began stripping the layers off, erasing all the lies I told myself and others."

STAND IN YOUR TRUTH

SIX

STATISTIC

Everyday I lived the life of a statistic, which was nothing more than a nameless item of collected information; a mathematical equation used to analyze what is happening in the world around us. This very information stated I was among: the 68% of children who grew up without a father; the 87% that were below the poverty line; and the 50% of those who were abused either physically, mentally, verbally and/or emotionally.

These mathematical equations and predictions would be easy if the data always sent a clear message, but the message is often obscured by variability. Growing up in the inner city of Philadelphia, statistics were not something we "majored in" or studied, but we understood them as the way our lives were 'meant to be lived'. By all statistical accounts, I should be dead!

But what statistics didn't show was how often I cried, how I never believed I would amount to anything, how more than 70% of my life (23 years) was spent believing everything that my circumstances stated either directly or indirectly to me. For those 23 years of my life, I walked around believing the statistics that told me I would probably add to the percentage of those who: would have a child out of wedlock; would never graduate from high school; and especially never attend college. You see, while I escaped the statistics of those around me and finally "made it out", I only made it out of my local zip code and physical location, but I was still a statistic.

Yes, I was determined to no longer be the one who "wouldn't amount to anything", because yes, I was the one who "made it out". But I was still a statistic in both mental and emotional capacities. I still thought I was nothing. I still believed everything those percentages and equations indicated. I was programmed to only see what the numbers stated because well, as we all know, "the numbers don't lie"...

I then became a new set of numbers. I was now amongst the 79% of females who had pre-marital sex, believing the person I gave my virginity to was going to be my husband. I was now apart of the 63% of females who had sex before turning 21 years old and was pregnant before the age of 25. I now was also just like more than 45% of young females who had an abortion. I had become a statistic. The very thing I tried my hardest to avoid was now my reality. How could this be? What went wrong? I left one set of numbers only to be forced into embracing a new set. There I was, still a statistic.

I focused so much on the negative statistics, that I didn't celebrate the positive ones. The positive numbers that indicated: how many times God covered me when I put myself in danger; when He provided for me when I had no food to eat; and most importantly, the number of times He had forgiven and redeemed me. The positive numbers also that indicated that I was amongst those who gave their life to Christ and who were now covered under his blood. The newest statistic stated that: I was amongst the 35% that grew up in a house with drugs but was not an addict; I was in the 4% of those in my immediate family to graduate and earn a college degree; I was the only one of those amongst my immediate family and friends to give the collegiate commencement address; and I am one of the 68% of black females who serve as a mentor and role model in their community.

The biggest status change is that I am an overcomer. God is a protector. You see, because of simple statistics I was conditioned to only look at the negative findings and focus on that data but never the positive findings and data! Today I can celebrate both sides of the scale, because it is in fact an indication that no matter what "they" say, no matter where you start, it's about how you choose to finish and what you choose to look at.

Based on statistical data and grouped analyses, this book should have never been written. Ha-ha! My daily reminder to think twice about statistics says:

*"**Do not put your faith in what statistics say until you have considered what they do not say**"*-
William W. Watt.

I am so glad that I am now a part of a new set of numbers where the equation always turns out positive.

MADE MOMENT

The moment I realized that statistical data had two sides and I understood that variables change, was the moment I knew that I could change my status. I had to change what I looked at, what I believed and how I lived. Every day I strived to be a positive number, while never dismissing the negatives that aided in where I am today. With a whole lot of help from family, much prayer and even more faith, I stand today beating the odds and rewriting history. To God be the Glory!

You too can rise above the statistics and change the variables in your life. The beautiful thing about variables is that they change and are likely to continue to change, which tells us that God can and will change your situation, if you allow Him to and embrace what He has for you.

"The biggest status change is that I am an overcomer. God is a protector."

Stop Surviving and
OVERCOME IT

SEVEN

DEFINED

We are often defined by or look for definition in things that occur in our lives. Sometimes we look to the people that are the most influential in our lives, and many times, we come up with the way we believe we should be. To be defined as or placed merely into a concept, thought or perspective, can be the most challenging thing in a person's life. It really places a lot of pressure on a person! Each of us have a set of things, events, experiences and possibly people that have unconsciously shaped who we are and our perspective on life. I'm a firm believer in allowing life experiences teach you, but not shape you. This was something that I had to really let soak in because as long as I could remember, I allowed people, situations, and circumstances to *define* me instead of adding to me. Unfortunately, I was eight years old when I first learned to allow the choices of others define me.

Growing up with both of my parents addicted to drugs took a toll on me, both mentally and emotionally. Seeing my mother use drugs at the age of eight did something to me. While I didn't know exactly what was taking place and going on, I knew in my gut that it wasn't right. I also knew that it was something I shouldn't let anyone know about.

So I did everything I could to keep people from knowing what was going on in my house and in my life. I felt that if they knew, they would judge me, not like me and I wouldn't be allowed to play with them. After all, "nobody wants a drug user's daughter around them or their children" right?

Well, a few years later this perspective was confirmed when one of my high school classmates, made a rap song about my mother buying drugs off of him and as if that wasn't enough, he performed his song in the hallway during the busiest time of the day. I was once again, "the drug user's daughter". I lost the name Yahshikiah, and was instantly diminished to just "the daughter of the customer" he rapped about.

Not only did these situations define me, they dictated who I was and what I thought of myself, how I interacted with people and how I spoke and talked to people. This was in fact my first defect; subconsciously at the young age of eight I began to allow the actions of others define who I was. I learned to lie when things didn't go according to the standard set in my environment and eventually I learned to succumb to the things around me. I started acting like my situations dictated I should. Numbness invaded me. I believed who they said I was and I believed that low and useless was all that I'd ever be. So why not just roll with the punches right? In that moment, I allowed my issues to become my identity. The scared and helpless eight year old, became the emotionless, angry teenager who made decisions out of pain, because that's the person I thought I was.

This was my struggle for a very long time and it wasn't until one day I thought to myself, "Where would I be if 'they' didn't do drugs? What if I didn't have to pick up their slack? How would it be if no one knew what went on in my house? What if I wasn't so angry?" Then, in a typical angry person fashion, I listed every place I could go and everything I could be if "they" were what I thought they should be and I didn't have to walk around with such a dark cloud over my head. Then something hit me! I could still be all of the things I desired to be. It wasn't up to anyone else but me. I didn't have a drug problem, so I shouldn't be ashamed or allow "it" to stop me. They were living the life they chose. And I allowed them to live their life and to take mine too! It wasn't fair to me or to them, because I resented my parents for what I thought they did to me. Now, I'm sure life would've been a lot different had they not been addicted to drugs, but that wasn't my life, it was a circumstance, a hurdle even...one that could be conquered.

Despite what I thought, my life is not now, nor has it ever been defined by circumstances of my past or my pain. It took me a long time to understand

and embrace this, but I did it with the help of Christ. He told me I was not an accident, that He created me in His image. So therefore I am beautiful, powerful, purposeful and chosen. I chose to walk in the defining beauty of Christ!

So many of us believe that we are what has happened to us, that we are the result of our parents' choices, and that our upbringing or lack thereof has made us. Because of this thinking, we set our value and worth on what we saw, what we heard or what was said to us. We then begin to react in an unhealthy way - a way that only hurts us. But what if I told you that you aren't the sum of your actions or the actions of others? What if you used your experiences as learning tools to assist you rather than define you?

MADE MOMENT

The moment I realized that the actions of others didn't define me, nor did they have any vote in my choices, was the moment I learned who I was. I removed all the negative thoughts, images and attitudes and replaced them with those of CHRIST - the ones that said, "I am fearfully and wonderfully made", "I can do all things through Christ who strengthens me" and "I am royalty". In that moment I began the process of discovering who I was without definitions I picked up along the way.

You too can rise above what has defined you, what has held you captive and what has stunted your own growth! No matter what your issues, situations and circumstances say, they do not define you nor are they your identity.

"Your Issues are not your IDENTITY…YOU BELONG TO GOD"

EIGHT

MY PAST

There once was this place I used to reside. I lived there for a very long time, well over ten years. When I first moved in, I could not for the life of me, understand how I got there or why I was even living in such a place. It seemed as if I just ended up in "this place". There was no notice, no packing, or even a conscious effort to be there...I was just *there*. As I looked around this place, nothing about it resembled me, who I was or who I was destined to be. This place had a lot of walls, so many walls that I would often lose my way. There weren't many windows in this place, but all I could remember seeing was gloom, sadness and pain. And then there was the smell. It was a terrible and awful stench. The smell that came from this place burned my nostrils and smelled of rot and decomposition, misery and despair. The very thought of this place makes my stomach turn. Where is this place you might ask? This place was located between death and destiny. This place was my past.

Every day I woke up in this place and listened to the same song, watched the same show and went through the same emotions over and over again. I was reliving my pain every single day for a little more than twelve years. I hated this place, but it became who I was, and my issues had in fact become my identity.

My emotions held me captive and I lived in that prison mentally, emotionally and sometimes physically. One week I would be so angry that it would make me sick. Then the next week I would completely suppress everything. I'd then go into a state of depression, avoiding everyone and every feeling, pretty much walking around like a zombie. The baggage was so heavy that it prevented me from moving, from loving and from being present. I grew to have a love-hate relationship with this place.

Bishop T.D. Jakes says something very profound on this,

"**When you hold onto your History you do it at the expense of your Destiny**."

That was exactly what I was doing. I held onto everything that happened to me and it robbed me of enjoying my life, learning who I was and loving me. In order to be different from and not resemble your past you have to go through the process. It's during the process that you will stand face-to-face with healing, freedom and deliverance. We must remove the bandages that we use to conceal the scars. The problem is that none of us want to confront the emotions or feel the pain that comes with removing the bandages. We keep ourselves locked in our past and pain, out of fear that someone might see the scars that are suddenly on display. However, when we keep and conceal our pain we are ultimately reproducing the pain over and over again. You will never conquer what you don't confront.

We all have situations in our past that have shaped us, scarred us or SCARED us, but in order to heal, be free and delivered you must take the bandages off. We all know that any wounds, scars or cuts that are covered for a long period of time run the risk of infection, and once infection is present, it spreads to other parts of the body if not treated right away. It's important to visit your past before it comes to visit you and infect who you are and where you're going. Making peace with your past is probably one of the most important journey's you will ever take!

Not only does it allow you to move forward and into your future, but it allows you to live in your truth and allow God in, to truly free you from bondage. Now for clarity, making peace with your past doesn't mean calling up an "old flame", going to the old hang out spots or calling those who've wronged you to cuss them out – no, that's not what I'm saying. I'm saying to truly revisit your past and take a detailed look at how it's hindering your growth and your future.

In my adult life I've noticed that my obsession with planning and doing things on my own comes from needing to have control. I have to feel in control because growing up I couldn't control my childhood or the things that occurred. I vowed that once I was able to take care of me, I WOULD. I hated the feelings of being let down and depending on others and most of all, *uncertainty*. My defense became taking control. As I began to understand how my past added to my present, I realized I needed to make a change, live in my truth and surrender every ache, wound and heartache to God.

Today, I realize that it's ok to trust the unknown and it's ok when things don't go according to plan because I'm not alone. I can depend on GOD because He will show up and show out in my life. His word tells me that He will never leave me or forsake me, so I no longer have to hold on and try to control everything out of fear of abandonment or being exposed. So I decided to make every effort to find my way out of that place.

MADE MOMENT

I realized that while I did not have control over the things that happened to me in my past, I did have control of what I did with the pain of my past. For so many years I put myself in prison and checked myself into that "place", because I chose to relive it every day. Once I realized I held the keys to unlock those doors, I freed myself. You see, God had already restored me. He had already mended my hurt and pain, but for some reason I decided to stay just a little while longer. Then one day I mustered up the courage to unlock the door, walk out and throw away the key.

"Our Past is just a place of reference for our Purpose"

NINE

TRUST ISSUES

Trust! That one word that has so much power, but brings about so many questions. Every single day we make choices about how much and who to trust. Sometimes we trust more than other times, when it seems to be needed most. I now realize that trust was always something I had a very hard time doing. Trusting anyone other than myself was just not something I did. For well over twenty years, I relied on myself. Taking care of my brothers and myself since I was fourteen years old, living on my own at the age of seventeen, and working full-time, all caused me to trust and rely solely on me. I had been the only person I could continuously count on, and while I've had help from family and friends along my journey, it wasn't consistent, so I learned to only trust me.

When a child doesn't receive adequate nurturing, affection and acceptance and similarly was abused, violated and mistreated, they will most likely find difficulty in establishing trust in others as an adult. Because of the inconsistency of my parents, and being abused by them throughout my childhood, I learned never to depend on anyone and that if people did in fact offer assistance, I should always be skeptical. I would think, "At what cost is this coming to me? How long will this last? What is this person's true intention, when I can not give back to them or be who they think I should be?" That became my mindset in every relationship I had with family, friends, boyfriends...everyone. It was the only defense mechanism I had and the only way I knew to protect myself. My relationships weren't healthy because all I could think about was people leaving me, so I learned not to get too close, not to let them "in". While I thought I was protecting myself, I was actually creating a hindrance. Not loving fully and not letting my guard down caused me to miss out on some very crucial and important lessons along the way.

Having trust issues caused me to not trust in God fully or be able to receive His blessings. I struggled with deeming myself worthy of his love, blessings and protection, because after all, everyone who was "supposed" to love me, had failed me. They either abandoned or resented me, so why would I receive what he had for me with open arms?

After years of doing things my own way, being hurt and not trusting, I have come to learn that the only consistent thing in my life is and always has been GOD. He has always been there for me, providing, protecting and loving me. God has had His hand upon me since the day I was conceived. And years later, trusting in Him has been the best relinquishment of power I have ever experienced. It is through Him, that I learned to trust - trust my family, friends and most importantly my husband. Because I relinquished my control and gave my concerns to God, I am able to be free and experience healthy and loving relationships. I've been able to reestablish the trust with important people in my life and I also have been able to attract trustworthy people into my life.

When we trust God with our lives, our hearts and our situations- it doesn't matter what man does or attempts to do because God is in control. Today I stand happy and safe in God. I am trusting of Him in every area of my life, my family's life and in your life.

" *In you Lord, I put my trust*"
Psalm 25:1

MADE MOMENT

Once I identified my biggest fears with trusting and realizing those fears could never kill me or hinder me from growing, I chose to be open to trusting. I am thankful that I no longer live in the bondage of my trust issues. I learned to trust differently. The example of truly trusting has been set and established by God. Trusting is a choice. It's something that you do. Your choice becomes your reality.   Becoming whole would not have been possible had I never made the choice to trust.

"You free yourself when you stop TRUSTING in man!"

TEN
IDENTITY THEFT

"It ain't what they call you. It's what you answer to"- W.C. Fields

One of the most frightening experiences of today is that of "Identity Theft". Why? Well, quite simply, most people who experience identity theft aren't even aware that they have been violated.

Identity theft is the fraudulent acquisition and use of a person's private identifying information. It's an invisible crime. Someone quietly steals your identity and uses it for financial gain. Diane Turner revealed that identity theft victims often 'show emotions much the way a trauma survivor would respond or somebody who was a victim of a different kind of crime such as home invasion or assault would respond'. So many of us are walking around not as victims of identity theft for financial

98

gain but **emotional identity theft**. We have allowed our issues to steal who God called us to be!

Emotional Identity Theft is the fraudulent acquisition and use of a person's emotional behaviors. Someone, or in our cases something, wrongfully obtains and uses our emotional data in a way that involves fraud or deception. It is when our pain, our rejections and ultimately the lies of the enemy violate us and attempt to steal our identity in Christ.

My entire identity had been wrapped up in my childhood trauma. Who was I without it? I lead with it. I introduced myself as such. I embodied the pain and allowed my issues to become my identity. I was a daughter of an addict, I was worthless, I was an accident, a mistake. Never mind what God said about me, because my issues spoke louder and they stole every promise that was etched in my heart. Those issues stole so much from me - my joy, my peace, my values, my purpose and who I was destined to be. I was blindsided by this robbery, not knowing when, who or how this had all happened. All I knew was that I woke up to an empty place in my heart. A place where purpose once resided, a place where love, laughter and joy were the accent colors. And so, I became a victim of emotional identity theft. I reduced every part of me to what happened to me. Just like identity theft, emotional identity theft leaves a scar. You become a victim, scared that you'll be robbed again, so you live your life in fear. You fear that it will happen again and you fear that everyone around you is capable of stripping you of your purpose. The number one emotional impact of identity theft is a sense of powerlessness or hopelessness. I was powerless. I knew what my identity was in Christ, but I believed I was disqualified from it because of my past.

The woman with the issue of blood lived 12 years in emotional identity theft and during that time she was helpless and powerless. She tried on numerous occasions to receive healing and a better life but to no avail. She spent countless amounts of time, energy and resources trying to receive healing. Her physical issues robbed her of a normal life, just like our issues have robbed us. During the time period in which she lived, a woman who was bleeding during her menstrual cycle was considered "uncleaned" and was prohibited from coming out in public. Now, this wouldn't have been a problem during a normal 3, 5, or 7 day span of a cycle, but the bible tells us it was twelve years! For twelve years not only was she in physical pain, but emotionally, mentally and spiritually she was in agony. Figuratively speaking, she couldn't assemble with other believers, she couldn't sing on the choir, go to the mall, or hang out with her friends because her issues robbed her of that.

" *There is a fine line between experiencing your pain and allowing it to become who you are* "

How many of us are living a life that is not what God intended? Have your issues caused you to be an emotional victim, perhaps, a completely different person? For twelve years, she fought with the thief, trying to prove that she was more than what they deemed her to be. She wanted back everything they took from her. And I know that she fought. Why? Because, for twelve whole years, even in the face of everything she went through, she kept trying.

She knew that she was more than what her illness stated and she refused to reduce herself to her pain. What about you? Will you believe the report of your pain or the promises of God?

God says you are:

- **The apple of his eye**   **Zechariah 2:8**
- **Justified and Redeemed**   **Romans 3:24**
- **Free**   **Galatians 5:1**
- **Chosen**   **Ephesians 1:4**
- **Accepted**   **Ephesians 1:6**
- **God's masterpiece**   **Ephesians 2:10**

In order for you to take back your identity you must first **change the narrative** - the narrative is the conversation you have within yourself. We hold mini stories about ourselves in our brains that we replay over and over again based upon our experiences. Because your pain has stripped you of your identity and your purpose, you've been replaying what it says about you instead of what God has proclaimed you to be. In order to believe something different, you must tell yourself something different. Pain and the emotions associated with it only last for a few seconds if we don't hold on to the narrative. I often wonder what the woman with the issue of blood said to herself the day she heard that Jesus was in town, knowing there would be thousands of people outside and that she was forbidden to come in public? How did the conversation in her mind or within herself shift for her to muster up the strength and courage to GET UP and get her healing? It is my belief that the conversation started long before Jesus came to town and that it started when she began praying and seeking his face. It began the moment she looked in the mirror and no longer saw defeat, no longer saw what they took from her but instead when she saw who she could be.

There was a decision made way before the act of pushing through the crowd. My crowd looked a little different from hers, but it started the same way. I made a decision that I would no longer rob myself of living a life of purpose. I decided that I had lived in fear, in pain, in doubt and in depression long enough, and that I would no longer reduce all that I was to my childhood, my parents, my poor choices in relationships and my pain. I was not my past, I was not what others spoke over my life, I was not my issues but, I was ENOUGH. Knowing that I was enough - enough for the healing process, enough for the journey, enough for this life, enough for everything that was promised to me, not only changed the narrative, but led me to decide to push through the pain and start from where I was.

Today is the day you start - not looking into the past, not waiting for the future, but starting where you are right now. You are no longer what your issues have said about you. Instead, **today** is the first day of the rest of your life. You have a new identity.

MADE MOMENT

The moment that I understood that my identity was not a reflection of what happened to me, was the day I was able to accept who I was. For so long my identity was wrapped up in my issues, my pain and what had happened to me. I thought that I was a victim but really, I was a survivor. I survived a devastating robbery and while I can't get any of the stolen goods back, I am okay because the loss of those items became the fuel that I needed to propel me into my purpose. My identity is what makes me unique - my characteristics, my strengths, my weaknesses, my gifts and my talents - basically everything that God created me to be is who I am. The moment we stop reducing ourselves to what happened to us, is the moment we find strength in BEING all that God created us to be. It happened TO me but it is NOT me.

"*First, you BELIEVE, then you BECOME*"

ELEVEN

RELEASING THE PAIN

Emotional pain is one of the hardest forms of pain to treat and to get over. This type pain is often the dictator to every portion of our lives. Each of us have experienced or are currently operating in pain, and while we all have pain, it's what we do with it that really matters. I've found that most people do two things with their pain: manage it or mask it, and for so many of us, it's the latter. We as human beings, especially women, have mastered how to hide - hide our feelings, hide our pain, and ultimately hide who we are. In hiding, we believe that it's better to sweep things under that invisible rug of our hearts, than to confront our pain. The concern that comes with "sweeping the pain under the rug", is that once the rug gets too much *stuff* underneath it, the rug becomes lumpy. This creates a painful visibility

108

and our everyday tasks become too hard to maneuver around because we keep tripping over all the pain that we've swept under that rug. If we hold onto the hurts and wounds of the past, we start accumulating emotional baggage; the dead weight of our old experiences.

My rug (a beautiful rug might I add) had far too much stuff underneath it and not only were the things buried beneath it beginning to surface, but the rug started looking dingy and began taking on the life of the stuff.

Managing any form of pain isn't an easy task, because it requires you to deal with it head-on. We are so hesitant to approach or release our pain because it requires that we open old wounds. But in order for us to be a healthy, whole and happy individual, we must confront our pain. We cannot conquer what we don't confront, nor can we release what we are scared to acknowledge. We will never operate in wholeness physically, mentally or spiritually if we keep our pain locked up. We run the risk of being emotionally toxic and those toxins will resurface in every area of our lives, if they are not released.

Releasing the hurt starts with identifying the hurt. You must acknowledge and identify your pain - no longer pushing it aside, acting as if it hasn't consumed you, altered you or made you different. When we identify the pain, we start the process of Release and Conquer. The first step is "to admit the problem" and the same concept applies when dealing with hurt and pain. There is liberty in being able to stand up and identify your pain. It's like finally catching the criminal who robbed you of something priceless and getting a call from the police station to come and identify the thief. You know that this will start the process of them being put away for life. How liberating is that?!

Freeing yourself of emotional baggage is the best gift you can give to yourself. Why? Because, when you don't release that pain, when you dwell on the past, it robs you of experiencing the gifts of the present. And it's in the present, the moment, the here and now, that you experience love, joy, peace, and happiness.

MADE MOMENT

Once I stopped holding onto my hurts and opened my heart, the healing took place. When my heart was open, it forced fear, doubt and hurt to leave, making a way for faith, love and happiness to move in and make a permanent residence. It was as if my heart had an "Aha!" moment and started beating to a different tune and allowing joy to flow from it.

"Freeing yourself of emotional baggage is the best gift you can give to yourself."

TWELVE

THE PROCESS

In order for anything to be purposeful, complete, and made whole it requires a process. A process is required to obtain a job, buy a house, go on a vacation and also to be powerful. We are eager to go through these types of processes as long as we're sure of the outcome and it doesn't require too much from us. When I learned and understood the significance of the process, it helped me to surrender and embrace my process. Everything that is GREAT has a process.

My process wasn't as straightforward as an application process - mine resembled more of a diamond making process. The diamond starts off as a mere piece of coal - a dirty, black, lump of coal. Coal is a rough stone, but has the potential to be a rare and exquisite diamond, if only it can withstand the process. When I researched what a diamond actually is, I found that it's an unbreakable and treasured gem. We should understand that just like that former piece of coal, we too could be something exquisite if we would allow ourselves to go through the process.

Everybody wants to "shine bright like a diamond" but nobody wants to get cut! The only way for a diamond to be flawless, rare, exquisite and to shine its brightest, is to be cut. There is an enduring process for cutting the diamond and it involves four important steps:

1. The first step in the process is called the **planning.** It is in this crucial step that the planner decides where to cut the diamond in order for it to be the most polished stone. Everything that we go through is to help us be our best and it was already a part of the plan to not allow our issues to kill us or overtake us but to shape us.

2. The second step in the diamond cutting process is the **cleaving** or **sawing.** This is when the

diamond actually undergoes the cut. Depending upon the roughness of the diamond, the decision is made to use a cleaver or to saw the diamond. Ouch! Sometimes what is weighing on us or the things we've picked up along the way, determine how we might be cut.

3. The third step in the process is called the **bruting.** During this step the diamond is rubbed up against another diamond. Once we are cut, we often need others who have "been there, done that" to help us shine, grow and be better. Isn't God such a gentleman to send us someone else who has encountered something similar to help us along the way?

4. The final but most significant stage is the **polishing**. It's in this stage of the process where the diamond gets all cleaned up and the foundation is laid for the potential of the diamond. After we are cut, we must be cleaned up and get prepared for our purpose. We must be reintroduced to the world because we no longer look like the dirty coal from the mine in which they found us, instead we are now exquisite and priceless.

The process is not to make you weak or to suffer, but to enhance who you are and assist you in becoming a treasured gem. We must understand that if any part of the process is negated, the diamond has to begin all over again. When we can come to grips with our lives and everything that we have the potential to be, then we can submit to the process. While I did not know my worth when I was going through the process, everything I went through prepared me for this very moment. I was bruised, but not broken – cut, but never cut-off! It was in the cutting, during the process, that my power was discovered. We can now thank God for the process and trust Him to make us complete.

MADE MOMENT

Just like that dirty piece of coal, I too had so much *stuff* on me. Looking at myself, I couldn't see the potential I had. All I could see was the dirt, the grime and the stains of my issues, but I'm grateful that God and others saw who I would become after the process. I am grateful today for my process and all of the pruning and picking that came along with it. It was in my moment that purpose was revealed and I found my voice - I am a Diamond, no longer in the rough.

"Everything that is GREAT has a process, don't negate YOURS"

THIRTEEN
FORGIVENESS

Every one of us has been hurt - hurt by the actions, words and decisions of someone close to us. These hurts have left each of us wounded with feelings of bitterness, anger and betrayal. Because of such negativity, forgiveness is often a very hard task to undertake.

Forgiveness is a "***shift in thinking toward someone who has wronged you***", says Psychologist Sonja Lyubomirsky. Forgiveness can be defined as the decision to let go of resentment, anger and thoughts of revenge as a result of a real perceived offense, hurt or wrong-doing against you. Now, before you decide to skip this chapter, hear me out, I haven't disappointed you this far... well at least I hope not! Smile ☺

Seriously, forgiving someone doesn't mean that you are dismissing a person from their responsibility of hurting you, nor does it mean that you are minimizing or justifying their actions. Forgiveness does mean that you are willing to release someone from having control over your emotions, without condoning or excusing what they've done. Most times we believe that forgiving means letting them "off the hook" when in fact, it's the total opposite. Forgiveness means that we acknowledge the hurt without allowing it or the person to control us. We must understand that we have to forgive the person, not the action. We must stop looking to blame the person more than we do the offense.

Let me clarify something I learned on this road, forgiveness is not reconciliation. These two are very different. Forgiveness is one person's inner response to another person's wrongdoing, whereas reconciliation is two or more people coming to a mutual understanding and level of respect for one another. Forgiveness is the only thing you can control. Forgiveness is a choice and is the ability to maintain control of your power, because when we don't forgive, we relinquish our power over to that person. We allow them to control who we are, what we do and say and even how we act.

Forgiveness is for you, not for them. For years I thought I would be "letting them get away with it" and I held myself captive because I didn't understand the concept of forgiveness. While I could never change the things that happened in my life, I decided to no longer allow the people who hurt me, to dictate my future or control my happiness. I noticed that whenever a person who hurt me came around, I was reminded of the offense and the hurt and betrayal, which would instantly put me in a sour mood. I can remember being at a party once, having an amazing time and suddenly a person who wronged me walked in, and my entire experienced changed. I relinquished my power to them over and over again - so much so that I was never in control of my life. That is no way to live. I hated being so full of anger and hatred. I would cry myself to sleep because I was so mad that I was so mad! I knew it was wrong and I hated that I couldn't control my own feelings.

Now, I've had some things happen to me that some might say are "unforgivable", like being thrown out of my brother's funeral, being told I should've been aborted and so many other terrible things. While these things are within in reason for a person to "stay" angry, it served no purpose for my life, as it kept me powerless and I became just as low as the people who hurt me. When we are unforgiving to people, we sometimes mirror their negative image instead of holding true to our actual good nature.

Once I realized I was powerless and began to resemble the very person who hurt me, I decided to walk in forgiveness. It was the hardest thing I have done to date, because it required so much work. Forgiveness for me was a gradual process. I didn't wake up one day and forgive everyone that wronged or hurt me. I had to consciously decide every single day to choose forgiveness. It required a new mindset, an "emotional bootcamp" if you will. Some days the training went well and others, I just cried, prayed and started over. The only constant thing was my decision to change my mindset and to try again. My constant reminder was thinking of the many things I had done, both knowingly and unknowingly to God, that hurt Him but He still forgave me.

Forgiveness brings about peace - a peace that allows you to go on with life in a happy and loving way. So, forgive them even if they never acknowledge the wrong or apologize, don't become who hurt you.

MADE MOMENT

It was in those moments when I began to resemble the people who hurt me that I knew I was headed in the wrong direction. Everything I despised, I became: rude, angry, disrespectful and bitter. I tried so hard not to *be like them* but I had begun to take on those very characteristics, ouch! That was my "Aha!" moment and the push I needed to push through and forgive.

We not only free ourselves from a life of destruction when we forgive, we break generational curses. We no longer leave a legacy of anger, resentment and unforgiveness, but instead we leave the legacy that God entrusted us to leave: peace, power, love and emotional well-being. Forgiveness is for you and those assigned to you. Remember this the next time you have a bad "forgiving" day.

"Forgiveness is for you, not for them."

FOURTEEN

ACCEPTANCE

"I love you". The first time I stood in the mirror and uttered those words, was at the age of twenty-four. That's right, it took me twenty-four years to come to a place of loving, accepting, and embracing *me*. How I arrived at this place is quite an interesting tale. It was in college after an ugly breakup with my then boyfriend/escape from reality friend/situation I ended up in person. He'd left my dorm room for the last time - well at least it wound up being the last time. I'm sure when he walked out the door to head back home, neither of us thought it would be the last time. After all, we danced this dance quite often. You know, the "I'm Not Dealing with You Anymore Shuffle" or the "It's Been Almost Ten Years, Should I Stay Two-Step". This particular time something was different, as we finished this dance...I knew that this would be the last dance I would accept from this dance partner. Our rhythm was off and we stumbled far too many times to make this thing work and quite frankly he wasn't a gentleman. I spent far too many lonely nights in his presence. I craved more. I wanted to do a new dance like the Tango or "The Wop". I think at that point I would have even accepted the Electric Slide. A good dancer I was though, knowing how to give my partner space, allowing him to take the lead and coordinate every step in my life. The problem with that was because of all the hurt, rejection and low self-esteem I had, I often picked the wrong "dance" partners. My pain led me to some dancers that didn't value the dance or me as their partner. I spent far too many lonely nights dancing with people who quite frankly couldn't dance at all or couldn't appreciate the *art* of dancing.

I looked for men to validate me, to give me the attention and acceptance that I desired from parents. I longed to be loved but unfortunately, I ended up dancing to the wrong tunes with the wrong partners.

For as long as I could remember, I felt rejected - rejected by both my parents, rejected by my family and rejected by my friends. My first memory of rejection from my own mother came around the age of 9 or 10 years old. I was playing with my cousin and didn't like something or didn't want to do something she was doing, so I went and told my mother (I was a bit of a tattle tale). She told me that I needed to "act more like my cousin" and went on to explain how she "wished that I was quiet, smart and responsible" like this cousin. The dagger I felt in my heart pierced me for years after that. From that brief but brutal encounter, I began to withdraw myself from everyone and everything. I started being by myself, even when there were other people around. I learned not to express my feelings because I would only be told to be like another person in the process. During that time, not only had the spirit of rejection entered my mind but *comparison* crept in. What a dangerous combination.

My father would then add to the rejection with his actions - I have such great early memories of my father. Up until the age of ten, I could remember him coming to get me and living with him, my step-mother and siblings. I felt alive, I felt included and that I mattered. It was my escape from what was really going on at my mother's house. And then things changed. I remember my father telling me he would come get me one particular weekend and take me to Disney World. At ten years old I didn't know that realistically, you can't travel to Disney and back over the weekend. So I waited and waited, but no daddy. No call, no message, nothing but my mother in my ear saying, "I told you he wasn't coming! I don't know why you love him so much!" Being a young girl, that was a lot to process. Why did my father not love me as much as I loved him? Was it something I did that made him not show up? Did he love my siblings more than me? More rejection, more comparison, more sorrow. What I didn't know at the time was that my father was at the beginning stages of addiction coming in and ruling him. While he once

129

was just dabbling in recreational drugs, he now was a full-blown addict and had no *control*.

Over the next five years I then began to seek approval from others thinking, "there must be something I could do to be loved." So I started making people laugh, while masking my pain. I started cooking, giving my money away and allowing people to use me all so that I could be accepted. The twisted message I received was that 'there was *something I needed to do*, to be accepted'.

For years after that I secretly battled with low self-esteem and questionable self-worth. I had issues as it related to love and being loved. On the surface I appeared to have it all together, one of the 'strongest young lady's you'd ever met'. I was very involved in high school. I was outgoing and had many friends but as soon as the bell rang, it was like the producer yelled CUT! The show was over and I could no longer pretend everything was ok.

No one knew I hated going home. No one knew I longed for love and affection. No one knew that I questioned who I was daily or whether or not God loved me. What was my purpose in life? I just wanted to be loved - truly loved by my parents and my family and I wanted love from myself. I thought I was an accident, a mistake. I couldn't have been on purpose the way that I felt and surely God didn't mean to create me! These were honestly my thoughts and I battled with this deep-rooted seed for years until one day in my frustration I questioned God and asked, "WHY ME?" And I can remember, clear as day Him responding, "WHY NOT? Why not you? Why wouldn't I love you, shield you and protect you during this difficult time? Why wouldn't I isolate you so that you didn't have to see or hear such negative things? Why wouldn't I make you strong enough to endure your current condition?" He then led me to read my first and now my most favorite scripture:

Then he taught me and he said to me, "Take hold of my words with all your heart; keep my commands and you will live" - *Proverbs 4:4*

I began to ask God to show me what it all meant and he led me to *Jeremiah 29:11*

" For I know the plans I have for you," declares the Lord, "plans to prosper you and not to harm you, plans to give you hope and a future"

Even though I didn't fully understand everything those two scriptures meant at the time, I recited them day and night, holding on to what God said.

I struggled internally for years, because I began to feel something different inside of me, but I couldn't verbalize it. Not knowing how to act upon what I felt, I reverted to what was familiar, searching in the wrong places for acceptance, dancing the dance of rejection, allowing it to lead me and guide me.

Then it happened. I cried, I prayed and I got up, locked the door, and decided I would no longer dance this dance with anyone else including myself. So with tears in my eyes, I walked in the bathroom, looked myself in the face and said, "I love YOU *more*. I choose YOU and we will get through this." For the first time in my life, I accepted me!

MADE MOMENT

Everything you've ever wanted is on the other side of fear. The evil spirits deposited in me and wanted me to stay in bondage,- not love. Rejection wanted me to continue to place blame on my parents and focus on what they were not, but the moment I chose me, was the moment I was able to see GOD. I chose to love me, accept me, and begin the process of wholeness. I now fully understand both scriptures and have made it my life mission to live out each of those scriptures daily.

"Everything you've ever wanted is on the other side of fear."

FIFTHTEEN

I'M FREE

"Freedom is what you do with what has been done to you."- Jean Paul Sartre

Oh to be F.R.E.E. - **F**inally **R**eleased from **E**xperiences and **E**vents that have paralyzed and broken me! As I closed my eyes, and exhaled, I released the last bit of the pain, past and power inside of me. I held onto pain, bitterness and anger far too long and was finally ready to experience freedom. Freedom is the greatest gift I could have ever given myself. To be completely naked and unashamed is the gift of freedom for your mind, soul and overall well-being.

To arrive at that place of being *F.R.E.E.* takes strength and courage. It requires that you fight through *you*, your thoughts, your attitudes, your hurts and your bitterness. When we think of the ability to free ourselves sometimes we make it harder than what it is. Think of a time when you try to open a jar that's extremely tight but you just can't get it. So you call for some assistance, the person comes in, loosens the lid for you and walks away. Your job then is to take the lid off, but instead you sit with the loosened lid and jar in hand, ready to be opened and everything in it released. God freed us the moment we came to him and accepted Jesus Christ into our hearts. He loosened the "jar" that held our pain and gave us the power to remove the "lid" and live in freedom. But often times we just sit there waiting for him to remove the lid for us. You hold the power to your freedom.

In order to be free, in order to live a life not bound by what was done to you, you must learn to manage it - manage your past and manage your pain. When I say "manage it", I mean to put "it" in its proper place. You have full control over what you do with the "lid" once God loosens the jar.

I understood that I didn't walk in freedom for over twelve years because I didn't manage what was done to me. I never took the lid off and I never let it go. Because I held on to the lid, I wasn't able to release my past. It remained locked in the jar of my heart, spirit and mind. Every time I had a moment to myself, I stared at the jar, wishing I had enough courage to remove the lid and empty its contents onto the floor.

Freedom came once I stopped staring at the jar and when I took the lid off and threw it away. The walk to the dumpster was the longest walk of my life, but it was the most fulfilling and liberating walk I had ever taken.

It's time for YOU to release yourself. It's time to free yourself and to forgive those who hurt you and who caused you pain. It's time for you to relinquish the resentment. It's time to take the lid off of that sealed container of pain that you buried so tight and so deep.

MADE MOMENT

Today, my smile is the brightest because of the freedom I have. God gave me freedom the moment I gave Him my life, but I never walked in it and I never acted on it, because I was scared. I knew nothing else but the bondage of my pain, but I gave myself the best gift ever - FREEDOM from myself. Everything you've ever wanted is on the other side of fear. Do not allow fear of "emptying the jar" to stop you from taking the lid off. It may stink and it may look bad, but IT IS WORTH IT!

"Freedom requires that you fight through you, your thoughts, your attitudes, your hurts and your bitterness."

SIXTHTEEN
GET UP

When I say GET UP, I'm not referring to just standing on your feet, although that's a good place to start. When I say GET UP, I'm also not talking about hanging out with someone as in "Okay, I'll get up with you later!" No, I'm speaking to your spirit, your emotions and your mental capacity. When I say GET UP, I am speaking to the core of who you are! GETTING UP is the courage to rise above the pain you feel inside. It's the bravery in making a decision to no longer live in fear, doubt, or the lies your situations have told you. Getting up is holding the little wounded girl's hand and whispering "you are ENOUGH" softly in her ear, as you wipe the tears from her eyes. The little girl is you...

Here's the thing, we all have fallen down due to a life altering situation that landed us in a painful pit, but you don't have to stay there. For so many of us the problem isn't that we fell, it's that we stayed down. We fell into an emotional hole and at first it's lonely, frightening and dark, but after a while we began to make it our home. That place that was once so scary and uncomfortable has now become our comfort zone. We've found familiarity in this place, because it's a reminder of our experiences and our disappointments and it serves notice that we can and will be hurt. So we trade bravery for hurt and comfort. You've set up camp and made a passing place your permanent residence. That emotional pit is not your home, nor is it where God intended for you to be. Your life has meaning and purpose, and that purpose is to be LIVED OUT, not locked up in an abyss of pain. The pain was never intended to imprison you but instead, to PROPEL you.

The Bible tells us in Proverbs 24:16 that "...*though the righteous man fall seven times, they rise again*". Another translation says they "GET UP AGAIN". No matter where life has taken you or what has happened you must get up. You were not designed to stay down. You have resilience, tenacity and most importantly purpose. So you have to get up. No, seriously, whether you've fallen mentally, emotionally, spiritually or all three, it's time to GET UP! So many people have gotten up and began walking in their purpose. You are no different, and it is not too late.

Getting up requires that you take action, that you give yourself permission to process your pain and to use it as your launching pad. Getting up requires a commitment from you that no matter how you feel, how dark it is, how long it takes, you will place one foot in front of the other and push yourself up and never look back! It requires that you say YES to your process, YES to your healing, YES to uncertainty and YES to no longer being complacent.

MADE MOMENT

"YES", changed my life. YES, is the reason I got up out of my pit - and let me tell you, it was a low place, and I was as low as I could possibly be. I was so deep in my pit that I didn't recognize myself, all I saw was darkness. I can remember being so deep in, that all I wanted to do was die, and I looked forward to the day it would finally be over. But one day in the midst of the darkness, something leaped inside of me, and at the time, I didn't know that it was my purpose. I didn't know how and I didn't know when, all I knew was that I wanted out and the first step in getting "out" was getting UP. So I crawled, cried, stumbled, scraped my knees until they bled, but I said YES! YES to lifting myself up to higher places and brightness! YES to pushing past the pain! YES to allowing God to remove every wicked stench off of me. So, when you hear me scream "YES!" throughout this journey, it is because YES changed my life. I will even go a pace further and say that YES carried me to the finish line.

"GETTING UP is the courage to rise above the pain you feel inside"

SEVENTEEN
MADE WHOLE

"*Honey I'm home!*" is what I exclaimed opening the front door. I inhaled and took in the scenery. This spacious, beautiful place was full of potential. Perfect. Just for me. The space I've always dreamed of! I window shopped here often and imagined hosting luxurious soirées here. Holding the keys to this space made it real and I knew I'd made the best decision ever. The process was excruciating, so many sleepless nights, much uncertainty and several moments of wanting to throw in the towel, but to stand here seeing the manifestation, makes all the hard work, sweat and tears, *worth it*. While I can still see remnants of the previous occupants, there are signs of renovations. The renovations add character and charm, which make me appreciate this place even more. I know the sweat equity is what makes it priceless. To arrive at the place where the stains of your past do not move you at all, the smell of your past is nothing more than an odorless breeze in which you can inhale and laugh at, is to be made whole.

For so long I misunderstood what being "**made whole**" meant. I confused it with healing. I searched desperately for healing over the past fiftieth-teen years. But what I was looking to heal were the surface problems, only those things that are seen. It's like painting over the stain on the ceiling from a leaky roof - it looks presentable until the next hard rain. I kept repainting, instead of tearing the ceiling apart and assessing whether it could be fixed or whether or not I needed a new "roof". Wholeness starts from within and it's not a quick fix. It is in fact a journey - a journey of faith, determination, trust and commitment. Transformation only occurs when we decide to become whole. No quick fixes, no over the counter "duct tape", but actually putting in the sweat and leg work, and understanding that a skilled contractor is needed because we cannot just repair what we have broken, nor can we make every area of our pain a "do-it-yourself" project. You run the serious risk of not becoming whole when you do it yourself.

We need to restore all past hurt and forgive. We need to face every buried emotion and ultimately deal with ourselves. Standing face-to-face with your truth requires faith - faith to be able to know something is wrong and also to know that it's not a sickness unto death. The woman with the issue of blood in the bible, shows us that although she bled every day for twelve years, she still believed she would become whole. I know this because the bible tells us that she sought assistance from everyone she could and she spent an enormous amount of money trying to get well. At any time she could have called it quits (and I'm sure she thought of it often), but she knew that wholeness was out there, so much so that she sacrificed her life just to meet Jesus. Women of that day and time were not to be amongst "the people" when they bled and because her condition lasted twelve years, she was isolated and ostracized but she was determined to get better. She crawled through the crowd and touched the hem of Jesus' robe and when he asked who touched him, she replied. Jesus said to her, "**Daughter, thy faith has made thee whole.**"

Are you brave enough to push through the crowd? Is your desire to live a life free from your condition, your pain and your past? At what cost will you gain your freedom?

It is in the pressure that you find wholeness. It is when we activate our faith and believe what we do not see that we can become whole from within, to not just receive healing but *wholeness*.

Just like that woman, I was determined that I would not die at the hands of my condition, I would not be defeated but I would press past myself, what I saw, what I knew and allow my desperation to lead me to Christ and not to despair. As I crawled amongst the dirt, the rubble and the mess, I knew this was not my permanent residence but an avenue I had to travel down to be made whole. I'm so glad I chose not to take a shortcut when I didn't know where the road might lead, but I'm grateful for every road worker and street sign that aided in my process. Today, as I stand in the renovated space in my heart, I see so much potential. I know where everything goes and I can now invite people in and not be ashamed of the buildup under the rug, because there are no rugs, just beautifully stained hardwood floors.

Today, I know who I am and can sit comfortably in the window of life, knowing my place, how and where I fit and what it took to enjoy the view. I am free, whole and ready to conquer the world. Again, I exhale and say, "***Honey I'm home!***"

"Wholeness is being brave enough to acknowledge the broken pieces, and finding the strength to be put back together"

EIGHTTEEN
HOME

As I look at my life, I am in a great place, a place of safety and security that I've longed for. My heart recognizes this place. A place is filled with love, assurance and intentionality. This place is home. Home is seeing the bruises of life but smiling because they're no longer opened wounds, home is texting my mother daily just to say hello without feeling resentment or bitterness. Home is making peace with my past and taking ownership of how I played a part in it. Home is choosing me, when everyone tries to guilt me into doing otherwise. My home is not a physical place but an emotional and spiritual oasis.

Settling into this place was hard, I thought that once I moved in, I would feel at home, but because I was so comfortable in brokenness, in pain I didn't quite know what to do in my new 'home'. I dreamt of this place, of hosting dinner parties and gathering just because. Here is was trying to get settled in, somedays it was hard, it was lonely...no pain, no rejection to talk to but I learned a new way of living. The way that God intended for me to live. I had

NINETEEN
HOW BAD DO YOU WANT IT?

"Anything worth having is worth fighting for"- Anonymous

The journey to wholeness requires that you want it, that you want to be free more than you want to be bound. It requires you to have more faith than you do fear, it requires that you make a decision. Our lives are the sum of decisions - whether good or bad and, whether they are our decisions or someone else's. You've read all about my pain, my struggles, my journey, now what? What will you do with what you know, what you've learned and what you've read? Will you be made whole? Will your faith ignite you or will your pain cause you to ignore it?

Wholeness is your birthright. It's yours and it's waiting for you to DECIDE. In John 5:6, Jesus saw a man lying there and knew he was ill for a long time, he asked him *"DO YOU WANT TO GET WELL?*...he knew that even though he was the chief physician, there was a level of accountability attached to healing and wholeness. You must DECIDE; decide if you're ready, if you want to put in the work. Decide if it's time. Decide if you'll get up and show up. The woman with the issue of blood stayed in her condition for over twelve years because something told her she had too, something kept her in this place, she tried small things, she went to "people" who she thought could help, but ultimately she had to purpose in her heart that WHOLENESS was available to her. She then decided that nothing would stop her from getting what she needed from Jesus. Even with all the physical pain, all the grief, the mental toll that it took on her, and all of the financial burdens, she still showed up to receive what was due unto her. When you want something bad enough, you'll do whatever you need to do to get it. By any means necessary...When was the last time you had a "by any means necessary" attitude? Have you approached your issue so forcefully that it had no choice but to change?

It's time to make peace with your past and walk in wholeness. In order to move forward in your purpose, you must make peace with your past, you must exchange pain for peace, past for purpose and paralysis for power! Everything you've been through was just the prerequisite to propel you to your purpose. Today is the day to give *you* a try, to push past every lie your pain, the enemy, or your past, has told you.

Are you ready to be WELL? To be WHOLE?

All the crying, hurting and all the pain you endured was not for you to JUST read this book, it wasn't for you to just know my story and sympathize with me, it is to be your launching pad into Wholeness. It was the leap you needed to move from your broken place. Now it's time to take your own journey from brokenness to wholeness. Be **MADE WHOLE**.

About the Author

Yahshikiah "Lady Yah" Hughes, is a high spirited, energetic, sought after anointed vessel of God who is being used as a Pastor, Transformational Speaker, Educator, and Trainer to transform lives and show people how to live in **purpose**.

A native of Philadelphia, Yahshikiah is no stranger to hardship, brokenness, and despair, but through perseverance, determination, and God, she has overcome obstacles and is determined to help others be healed. Yahshikiah dedicates her life to seeing others go from pain to purpose, doubt to destiny and victim to victor. Because of this she founded Made **for Purpose LLC**, a non-profit organization designed to uplift, encourage, and empower women of all ages, backgrounds, cultures and socio-economic statuses to "**BE MADE WHOLE** and **WALK in PURPOSE**". Through seminars, conferences, writings, and community outreach, **Made for Purpose** desires to bring healing, inspiration, and purpose to everyone.

Additionally, Lady Yah serves as Assistant Pastor alongside her husband, Kevin Hughes Sr., Founder and Senior Pastor of **Kingdom Vision Family Worship Center** of Dover, DE. Serving diligently throughout the entire ministry, Lady Yah has a heart and passion for people, especially women. She directly oversees the administrative arm of Kingdom Vision, the Youth and Children's Ministry, the Women's Ministry and the Outreach Ministry.

While all of this brings her great joy, her greatest accomplishment is that of being a wife to her amazing husband, Kevin Hughes, Sr. and their children.

Resources

Because Wholeness and Emotional wellness is not designed to be a one-time experience, I've put together a few additional resources that will assist you with not only being but staying WELL.

Wholeness Resources

Join our email list : www.madeforpurpose.org

Enroll in our signature course MADE WHOLE a 4 week intensive program that is infused with biblical and counseling practices. This course includes weekly virtual classes, a workbook, one on one coaching session and access to a private community for support.

Email *info@madeforpurpose* to enroll.

Become a member of Made for Purpose and gain access to monthly trainings, events and community of like-minded women. **www.madeforpurpose.org**

Book your Coaching Session with Yah Hughes, M.Ed email **yah@madeforpurpose.org**

Made in the USA
Columbia, SC
30 January 2018